DAVID: I think, probably like in C
science, the science of textual crit

It's a very exact science, and text
archaeologists. They look at all th
all that and try to get their best sh... ... .

I don't know if you used to listen to Terry Wogan on an early morning programme on Radio 2, but he always used to show his listeners something, and I'd like to show our listeners a Greek New Testament! Here we are, Jerry, a Greek New Testament. I open it at John chapter 8, and lo and behold, there's the Greek bit at the top. But there's a whole two-thirds of the page, which is just other variations, other readings. And the textual critics have shown us their evidence, they've said, 'Look, this is our best shot at the original, but here's the evidence – you check yourselves.'

And so, you can rely on it, and the fact it was 300 years afterwards, 400 years afterwards, well, that was the way with stuff in the olden days when they were copying. For instance, Caesar's *Gallic Wars*, which he wrote at the time of invading Britain in 55 BC . . . the oldest copy we've got is from 900 AD, a thousand years later. So, that's how it went. The Gospels were not texted directly from heaven.

BRENDAN: Well, I've got to confess that I'm a Roman Catholic of a certain age, brought up in the '50s and '60s. I think back to my very standard Catholic childhood and home, where we said our prayers and we went to church on Sunday.

There was a Bible in the house, but we very rarely consulted it. So, my kind of native Christianity was the parish, of the community, the family, of not quite doing what one senior Thompson told us to.

But Catholicism of the '60s and '70s, it wasn't a religion of the book in the same way as I'm aware that it was for my Protestant friends, and as it is more and more the case for younger Catholics.

That *primacy* of text, that preoccupation, that *starting point* as a word, as a book, isn't the place where I've ever started when I'm thinking about what's the truth of Christianity. It's a person, it's not some fixed script, at least that's always how it's been for me. So, these kind of things, so they're intriguing, they're interesting. But I kind of shrug a bit, you know?

OLIVIA: I was similarly shocked to know there was 5,700 copies, I have to say. But, when I looked at that, I thought that the fact that there are so many copies, perhaps is not that important. I think what *is* important is what each of those copies *point to* – the overwhelming truth for me of the story of God and his overwhelming love, overflowing love for man. And that for me is the *truth* of the gospel? Basically, that man is sinful, that there's a penalty that needed to be paid, that it was impossible unless God did it and stepped in to pay that penalty. I think that those are the truths that those 5,700 copies attest to, and that this truth changes everything.

[3]
JERRY: David quickly homes in on one episode, which most of the 5,700 copies omit, namely Jesus being forced to judge the woman caught in adultery. He quotes the former Archbishop, Rowan Williams, that despite the weakest manuscript evidence, it gives the strongest picture of Christ. What shocks our panel most about this episode?

DAVID: Well, it's clear that Jesus sends every lynch mob or rather every stone mob packing. End of.

And there's nobody in his eyes beyond forgiveness, beyond redemption, beyond acceptance. And so, that's quite shocking because sometimes people like to put a limit on Christ and his love and set a limit.

Rowan Williams again. He said, 'Look, if you want to wall yourself into a ghetto of your own prejudices, just peep over the wall. And on the other side of the wall, you'll see Christ himself waving at you.' And I think that's a good sort of correction, really.

BRENDAN: I'm a journalist. And what never shocks you is seeing how, when something happens, people take their response to what they see in front of their eyes from the other people standing around.

The woman taken in adultery was seen by a number of viewers, observers, men I think, as it happened. And you can sense in that story – you don't have to be there to know this – that they were looking at each other and taking their interpretation from what the group, what the herd, what they were judging. And that's completely unsurprising. We're all aware of that, that dynamic.

And it very quickly often becomes a common sense of horror, of there's us, the righteous, and there's that person over there, who's the sinner, and our purity and goodness comes from the fact that we're not like them, because that's a classic dynamic of this story. And every time that plays out, Jesus punctures it. He just finds the words that deflate the whole scenario. It's not a tit for tat from what the other people are saying; it's not a reaction against it or a nodding an agreement with it. It's a completely fresh take on what's happening.

OLIVIA: Simply, that she was caught in the very act of adultery. Now, I have always thought when I read that Scripture, who was watching? How did they catch her in that act really? What it draws me to though is how Jesus navigates the situation and how really, she was condemned, so her righteous execution was warranted according to the law.

But Jesus navigates that by asking some really challenging questions and then changes her execution into a place for freedom, starting with the very people who were probably ready to pick up the stones to stone the woman.

And it says that, you know, the oldest one was the one who left first, you know, that they . . . He said, who's the one who's without sin cast the first stone, and the one who's the oldest thinks, you know what? No, I'm not gonna do this. And he walks away followed by his younger contemporaries.

So, I think that's the thing that shocks me most, is that Jesus intervenes in this. But it's just a fact that there are these righteous people, lovers of the law if you will, who are bent on making examples of people and this woman was one of them.

[4]
JERRY: Later on in the session, David wonders whether the book of the Law, which roundly condemned that adulterous woman, really was found beneath the Temple during the reign of Josiah or was actually planted by him and his cronies to bolster their manifesto. If such an ancient book of the Law were discovered under Westminster Abbey today, what would it say?

DAVID: I hope it would say, let us be inclusive. Let's make sure that no child goes to bed tonight, frightened, or hungry, or unclothed. But I suspect if it was, quotation marks, 'found', it'd say something like, 'Thou shalt agree with Brexit', or 'Thou shalt disagree with Brexit', or 'Thou shalt agree that asylum seekers should be sent to Rwanda', or 'Thou shalt support austerity'.

It's an intriguing game, and, you know, it's an intriguing idea that Josiah invented the law rather than found it. But who knows?

BRENDAN: I probably wouldn't feel curious enough to go and take a look. It wouldn't be of that compelling interest to me . . . what the text says, it's, you know, an interesting archive, it's a box of old postcards. If we lost the box, if we lost the words, if that text, that document, somebody found it, then somebody came along and said, 'Oh actually, it's like Hitler's diary, you know, it's not authentic, it's not the real thing.' Or it was the real thing. I'm not sure it would make that much difference whether it was Hitler's diary or Hitler really wrote it. The gospel is, you know, the life of Jesus, his followers, that's the story and the history. And that's what we follow.

[5]
JERRY: David uses the term 'healthy uncertainty' when handling Scripture, and any absolute text or speech which claims to have divine credentials. I asked our panel, is that a good rule for life?

DAVID: I think it is. I was lucky with my secondary school here in Scarborough. And all my teachers encouraged me, encouraged us, to doubt everything. 'Don't take anything as read. Question everything, even us,' teachers said, 'even us.' And that stuck with me for life, and both in faith and science, in my faith studies and science studies. And I think it makes life fun because if you get beneath the veneer, you start looking at the really big things and interesting things. And I think, you know, dictators love blind acceptance. And to actually question, even faith, I think, is healthy.

BRENDAN: You're always, I think, you're back and forth between the certainty of who you are, what you stand for, and the uncertainty of gosh, how do I address this particular situation? So, I think it's a beautiful way of putting things, lovely phrase.

OLIVIA: I think I struggled a little bit with the term, 'healthy uncertainty', but I certainly knew where David was coming from. And he gave a really good example.

And I've come across that, as both the pastor and the minister, of people telling me, 'Well, God has said this.' And I've always been someone who, once people tell you that, it shuts down any argument at all! You just . . . there's no comeback.

I also think when it comes to the Bible, that we have to be really careful how we handle the Scriptures anyway. We can't take everything as being absolutely *the* qualifying thing because clearly the Bible is written with lots of symbolic language . . . it's a Bible. The Bible is a number of books, not just one, but there are certain truths that sign, that are signalled all the way through.

So, I do think that, when it comes to healthy uncertainty, that it depends whether we're talking about ourselves and what we're trying to discern of the Bible, and/or seeking the truth of what the Bible has to say about a particular passage or a particular topic of its own.

[6]
JERRY: David ends the session by quoting Sebastian in *Brideshead Revisited* – that he believes in nativity stories because they're a lovely idea. I asked our panel which gospel stories are lovely ideas which hearten them.

DAVID: Well, I think the parables for, you know, the first example, the parables are Jesus' lovely ideas, put into words, and they both hearten us, but also disturb us. Think the parable of the prodigal son, a lot of disturbing stuff there.

Number two, the healings, I think, are lovely ideas put into practice. Particularly the story of Jesus healing Jairus' 12-year-old daughter, where Jesus gets to the house and she's died, and all the mourners mock Christ for daring to think that she can come back again. But he brings her back. And that always brings tears to my eyes. And finally, a lovely story, come to life really, is the wedding at Cana, where you've got disaster of disasters: the wine runs out. A dry wedding of all things! And Jesus, spurred on by his mum, produces 180 gallons of extra wine, and it suddenly becomes a wedding of joy rather than misery.

BRENDAN: Again, this perhaps is a journalist's answer, but the gospel story of Easter morning when Peter and John . . . they hear from Mary Magdalena that Jesus has risen.

She's the first apostle of the resurrection. The boys hear the news and they . . . the report is that we hear in the Gospels, that they run to the tomb. And it's just you can see them! What's going on? They run to the tomb. And again, this is one of the reasons why I believe this story, because I know how people write and remember stories. And if you remember that story, John runs ahead; he gets to the opening of the tomb first. And he looks in and he sees that there's no body there. You can see the discarded linen. And then, puffing up alongside him, Peter arrives. It's always the detail that brings you to the place, that kind of tells you this is how it happened.

And that's exactly the kind of report that, when people breathlessly tell you what happened. 'He got there first! He looked in! And I was just stunned there, stunned! And then Peter came in; he came to see, he went in!' And I've always thought, you know, I think, you know, when you, again as a journalist and somebody who's on the phone, listening to people describe things, you kind of know when they're making things up. But that one has that ring of truth because of that detail. So, I love that one.

OLIVIA: So, three gospel stories that I think are lovely ideas which hearten me . . . is . . . probably the first is the parable of the lost son or the prodigal son in Luke 15. I love the story of the father waiting for his lost son to come home.

The second one is the story of Jesus walking on the water, in the storm, and Peter's boldness when he sees Jesus walking across to him and saying, 'Well, if it's you, just ask me to come', and Jesus says, 'Come', and he does so. Love that. That heartens me, that speaks to me so much.

And the third one is the woman who's healed of the issue of blood. And I particularly love her boldness in coming out. I mean, she, you know, she had an ailment that would isolate her and take her away from society, but she comes out and she touches Jesus, hoping that he won't notice. Her faith and her boldness is just amazing. So, those are the three ones, very quickly, that hearten me.

JERRY: More of that next time. That's the end of Session 1.

[7]
Session 2
STRANGERS IN THE NIGHT . . .

JERRY: At the beginning of this session, David points out that Matthew, Mark and Luke's Gospels have a very close literary dependence. So, what's going on? David first, then Brendan then Olivia.

DAVID: Well, the literary dependence is there, take it as read. Or written. I think the most popular theory, the latest theory, is Mark was the first Gospel. Quite short. And then Matthew and Luke copied from him, but introduced their own material, which was peculiar to them, but also had some shared material which Mark hadn't got. And that's how it worked out.

That sort of I think, as I said, that's the most popular theory, the latest theory. It works pretty well. But, if you look at an actual example, say the parable of the wicked vineyard tenants, which is there in all three Gospels – Matthew, Mark and Luke – in quite a lot of that, Mark looks like the earlier version, but in some bits, he starts looking a bit more developed than Matthew or Luke.

So, it doesn't quite work; it's obvious something's gone on, but precisely what's gone on . . . you get lots of theories, but nobody's ever come up with the absolute sort of absolutely convincing one.

BRENDAN: As we know now, I'm a journalist and the editor of *The Tablet.* It's a Catholic weekly newspaper. And it's pretty much stopped now, but for a long time, there were other Catholic weekly newspapers – they've all stopped publishing, I think Covid did for them – *The Universe, the Catholic Herald* – and we all had a slightly different kind of theological flavour, if you like. And one thing I would say to people, who want to know what's going on in the Catholic world, is that obviously, you know, subscribe to *The Tablet.* But read the *Catholic Herald,* read *The Universe.* Same way – I don't know about you, but I read *The Guardian, The Times, Telegraph* . . . Each one of them – they're all good journalists doing their best to tell the story as they see it, unadorned, if they're serious journalists. They're trying to give you the news.

But they come from different positions as we all do; it's inevitable. And, in order to find out what's happening, get a better sense of it, it's always better to read more than one story, more than one account of what's happened. That helps us.

Now, I'm not comparing Matthew, Mark and Luke to *The Guardian*, *The Times* and *The Telegraph*. But the idea of three synoptic Gospels, and they do look as if they can't both be true, they're giving slightly different accounts of things, I think it's a fantastic gift, actually, that we've got three different newspapers, three different Catholic newspapers (or used to have). And three synoptic Gospels. It just . . . again, it seems to me when I read them, it makes them more convincing, more persuasive. And it also guards you against having too simplistic an understanding of what gospel truth means.

OLIVIA: Although there's no evidence to substantiate which of these three Gospels was written first, I like the idea that Matthew, Mark and Luke have a story that they're telling that correlates with each other, that's collaborative. John, on the other hand, completely seems to have skimmed all of this, and chosen to skip, or may have chosen to skip, some of the information that's already covered by Matthew, Mark and Luke, but fill in the important gaps, as he saw it, by providing new material. And that heartens me, in a way, because I think John, being the disciple that Jesus loves, had witnessed first-hand some of the things that Matthew, Mark and Luke may not have seen. So, he includes things, like, you know, Jesus' early ministry, the first miracle at Cana with turning water into wine.

And so it may be that that's what's going on there, that he's actually seen because I think John's Gospel was written a little bit later than Matthew, Mark and Luke. He may have very well read, or at least had the first draft if you will, of what they've written and thought, 'Well, actually I want to tell a different story', and you'd expect it to be slightly different because of John's close relationship to Jesus as well, and being the only disciple that was alive at the time of him writing that.

[8]
JERRY: Talking of contrasting views, David mentions the wedding at Cana, with Jesus being off with his mum when she pointed out that the wine had run out. Surely Jesus had a wonderful relationship with his mother: 'Mary was that mother mild, Jesus Christ her little child', and all that. So, what do the panel think?

DAVID: I think we have to be careful to read the Gospels and not be influenced by carols – that's by Mrs C. F. Alexander, *Once in Royal David's City*. And it does say in St John's Gospel, Jesus rounds on his mum and says, 'What is there between you and me, woman?'

And the only other time that phrase is used in the Gospels is when the evil spirits say to him, 'What is there between you me, Jesus of Nazareth?' So, it's a pretty insulting . . . he rounds on his mum pretty insultingly. It is there in Matthew, Mark, Luke . . . there's an incident where Mary and the family come to take Jesus home because they think he's gone off the rails, being a wandering preacher, and they come to try and take him back to Nazareth to be a carpenter, safe at home again.

And Jesus isn't pleased with this. And they say to him, 'Oh, your mum and your family are outside coming for you.' And Jesus says, 'And who is my mother? And who are my family? Those who hear the word of God are my true mother, my true family.' So, that's pretty insulting there.

So, obviously there was an edge with every child, growing apart from his parents. And, you know, it's there. We can't airbrush it out. And sometimes, I think, we actually have to read the Gospels rather than go along with other sort of ideas.

BRENDAN: Well, I think we'd all recognize that story of the young son being quite snappy with his mother – we've all been there, and we'd probably all come to think later, when we look back on how we spoke to our parents a bit, 'Gosh what a plonker I was at the time!' And that's just a completely natural family dynamic. It seems to me that we're all dependent on our parents when we're young. We all hate being dependent precisely because we're young, and so we're always irritated and cross all the time. That's just the story of children and their parents. And again, that seems . . . I love that because he snaps at his mum, he says 'You know it's a wedding, what do you want?' And then he does what she says! But that to me, that example, that little exchange, just feels so familiar and authentic, and that's what love looks like in every family. It's a great story.

OLIVIA: I think I agree with David that Jesus is distinctly off with his mum. I think, you know, if I was there, I'd be saying, 'Oh, don't be so rude to your mum!'

But I think there's so much that's unwritten . . . that Mary knows who her son is. She knows that this child is a supernatural child, but not only that, but that he is God. And although Jesus sounds terse, and has said, 'Well, look, what's this got to do with me?', and certainly, 'What's it got to do with you, woman?', the use, the use of the term 'woman' . . . And I'm sometimes wondering if we are reading that in our modern-day parlance as to what it may have meant to Jesus and his mother then.

But what I love is what it goes on to say, is that Mary says, 'Do whatever he tells you.' It's almost as if she ignores his terseness. She says, you know, 'Whatever he tells you', to the servants, 'do it.' And that's where he performs his first miracle.

But I'm also reminded of who's writing this story and it's John, and John is there and he's witnessing Jesus' first miracle. And again, the relationship that John has with Jesus, to me gives him a unique perspective on all of this.

I love that miracle because it's just so random! So, I don't know what's going on, but certainly we're told at the end of that the disciples started to look at Jesus a little bit differently, you know, as you would do if someone, the Son of God, turns water into wine.

[9]
JERRY: In his text, David says that in urging Nicodemus to be born again, Jesus is demanding Nicodemus breaks with his past and expectations and dares to go for a moment of discontinuity. Are there any such moments in our panel's lives?

DAVID: It's a bit of a trademark with me, in that, as a bishop and former parish priest, I've gone to lots of meetings, lots of interviews. And at meetings, you know what it's like – people talk on and everything, and it's all the status quo and it has quite a momentum. Often, I cut across that, and I take my cue from Jesus when he was talking to Nicodemus. He cuts across all the waffle with his going to the heart of things. And so, I do that in meetings.

Personal moments of discontinuity . . . Well, I suppose getting married, getting ordained, having a child, are moments like that. They say that having a baby in the house is the best example of minority rule that you know, and that's a moment. So, all people have them, and you embrace them and move on.

BRENDAN: I'm 68 now. And I remember when I was 60, I thought I'd just about worked out what was the right kind of way of living that suited me, and it was about friendship and plenty of time for solitude, silence, lots of that. And I just met somebody then, and things got out of hand quite quickly. And it's almost a few weeks later where she said to me, 'We're pregnant.' And before the end of my sixtieth birthday, I was a father, and remarkably quickly as another two children came along, second and a third. So now, I've got no solitude. No silence. No order. All the things that I just gradually kind of found that these were . . . this is my metier, this would suit me, were completely overturned. And all the books are completely in the wrong order, all the records or cassettes all neatly made up . . . they've been turfed around by silk ties, covered in jam. And what you learn, I think, a lot of us learn, if you had these unwelcome, unexpected interruptions, is that it's not so bad. And you suddenly discover that we're such mystery to ourselves, what we think we are, what we need . . . we get these discontinuities, these total disruptions, and you find yourself in a place you never expected to be. And it's like, it's lovely! It's not . . . we're much more frightened of change, disruption than we need to be.

OLIVIA: Yes, I've had lots of moments of discontinuity, but I think the one that I would . . . that I think is probably best expanded upon here is becoming a Christian. Because I was, I would say, someone who loved going to church as an Anglican, brought up in the Church of England.

And so, I loved the religiousness of that, the certainty and knowing the rituals, the words, the lovely songs. And then coming, quite dramatically, to a decision because I went somewhere else – not outside of Anglicanism – I just went to a church that had a different way of doing and looking at the Gospels and really came face to face with someone, a preacher if you will, who asked me, and asked of his audience, to make a decision for Christ.

That had never been asked of me before by my vicar, who was a very tame, benign individual. And here I am being asked to make a decision, and making my faith something tangible, and inviting me then to discontinue my old way of, if you like, 'doing God', to be a person who's filled with faith, who's asking me to put my personal faith, not only in a confession, but in a *person*. And that moment, I think, is a moment of discontinuity between the way I did religion then and between the way I did it afterwards.

[10]
JERRY: **From birth now to the subject of death, which is surely the ultimate moment of discontinuity. David writes that in his conversation with Nicodemus, Jesus flags up that his moment of glory is not going to be his resurrection, but his crucifixion. Surely crucifixion is just horrible, obscenely horrible?**

DAVID: Absolutely. I absolutely agree. It's the worst death, the worst torture. And yet, and yet, we have crucifixes and crosses in the heart of every church, at the heart of our worship. People wear them around their necks. And what's going on there? Well, I think it's all due to John, in his Gospel really, that he dares to say that, rather than crucifixion being terrible, this is the moment of greatest glory for Jesus.

And you do get it in the other Gospels. You get the centurion, who would have seen a lot of deaths, he'd witnessed a lot of crucifixions, and yet he says, 'Truly, this man is the Son of God.' There's something in the way Jesus dies that makes him realize that here is God, in all his fullness. I think St Paul said, 'When I am weak, then I am strong.' And that's the heart of the gospel, that the crucifixion says something massive about God being present in suffering, God being present when things happen to you, rather than when you're in control.

BRENDAN: Crucifixion, and all the shame and humiliation that came with that particular crucifixion, is horrible. I suppose, again, it's things that we learn . . . is that there's no joy, there's no glory, without pain. There's no life without death. And there's no light without darkness, and crucifixion is the greatest darkness, but it's what, I think, what we believe makes the brightest light possible. Again, it's one of those mysteries, isn't it? There's no point, now, never embrace suffering and think it's great for its own sake, 'cause it isn't'. Suffering is bad, awful, but it might be necessary for life to be large and rich, and for the light to really shine brightly.

OLIVIA: Of course it is! We all know that you only have to do some reading on the history of crucifixion, and you know that the Romans, who instituted that, were . . . they were just looking for the most barbaric way of someone dying, perhaps to teach people a lesson. And yet, the crucifixion is obscenely horrible, it is, but for the Christians who believe, for people who place their faith in God, the crucifixion – and the resurrection – is absolutely front and centre of our faith. It's a fulfilment of prophecy. It's what Jesus has been . . . had been trying to tell his disciples and getting his disciples to understand – that he had to die. And maybe they thought, yeah, well, what kind of death is that?

But to be crucified, it's horrific. But it was important because the purpose of the crucifixion was to take away the guilt and shame of sinners. And it reminds us that it's to reconcile us to God, that by his grace we can live with him forever. So, it was a necessary price to pay, but yes, I agree it was obscenely horrible.

JERRY: That's the end of Session 2.

[11]
Session 3
THE WINNER TAKES IT ALL

JERRY: David starts this session by comparing two weddings, one set in Matthew's Gospel and the other at Cana, at the beginning of John's Gospel. Which wedding would our panel prefer to go to?

DAVID: For the moment forget wedding and think services or equate the wedding in Matthew and John with services. Which service do you prefer? If your service style is Matthew's wedding, then nobody comes, then the people who are strong-armed in are told off by the king/minister for not having quite the right attitude, not looking right.

So, that's Matthew's wedding, equating it to a service. Equate John's wedding to a service and you've got, suddenly, 180 gallons of extra wine, the most gorgeous wine in the history of the world, and everybody goes home drunk on Christ.

Which service do you prefer? You prefer the second one: it's joyous, rather than miserable. And you know, I've observed a lot of services over the years. Sometimes people come out of church looking more miserable than when they went in and that's quite a result! But they should be coming out, drunk on Christ; they've been partying with the Son of God, and they should come out thrilled.

BRENDAN: Well, I suppose, like most of us, I'm astonished at the idea that anybody would be daft enough to turn down a wedding invitation. I think weddings are always great! And the idea of people being invited and not turning up is a bit baffling, and the reaction of the host to bring in people, go out to the streets, bring people in, is delightful. But, I think, doesn't he kill the people . . ? That's possibly going a bit far, and I think the guys who come along who aren't wearing the dinner jackets and properly doled up, they get turfed out. So, that's perhaps the kind of wedding where I wouldn't be too disappointed if I hadn't been invited to that one. The wedding at Cana, well that does sound a hoot, you know. And they say the best wine was kept for the end. So, that would be the wedding, the wedding for me.

OLIVIA: I prefer the wedding at Cana, and I like it because it . . . the miracle of it being Jesus' first miracle was just so random! It's not like any of the other miracles that he did around healings or restorations or miraculous raising to death. No, here is Jesus, the Son of God coming out, making his debut. And turning water into wine! And not just ordinary wine, but the best wine that there ever was. And it was just a time of sheer joy.

It's also the disciples' first outing, and their experience of Jesus is where Jesus seems to have been goaded by his mother to say or do something about this. So, I love the miracle of the wedding at Cana. I do love that, that's my favourite one.

[12]
JERRY: Reflecting on Christ overturning the tables in the Jerusalem Temple, David wonders about him physically turning up at our places of worship. What would happen?

DAVID: Well, there's a joke, isn't there, about a vicar getting his church ready on a Saturday night, and his assistant comes up to him and says, 'There's a bloke at the back who's just come in. It's a tramp, but he says he's Jesus. What do you think?' And the vicar turns round and looks the tramp up and down and says, 'I don't think he is, but just in case, we're better look busy.'

And that's the problem, I think, we're probably too busy. Faith is too busy, and I think if Christ broke in now, he'd tell us to sort of shut up and move on from all the complications because, I've said it quite a lot in sermons and during church services, I don't think Jesus ever intended this to be so complicated.

So, he'd simplify us. He didn't give us a code of instructions; he gave us a meal. Archbishop John Sentamu, former Archbishop of York, used to say that the Church has the engine of a lawn mower and the brakes of a juggernaut. All sorts of reasons why things can't happen. I'm Church of England and Anglican. And so many people in the Church of England are Angli-can'ts rather than Angli-cans!

And I want things to happen. I think if Jesus came today, he'd want things to happen. And so, he'd make us have the engine of a juggernaut and the brakes of a lawn mower, and I think that would be just liberating.

BRENDAN: I'd be completely terrified if he came to my parish in Shepherd's Bush, or if he turned up at *The Tablet* office. Visit from the boss! What would we . . . what might he say? He'd obviously be appalled and we'd obviously . . . this is always the difficulty or the tension that we're strong on, because of course, we would say, admit that we'd made a complete mess of everything. We hadn't lived up even two percent of the way we hoped we would as good disciples. We've made a complete and total mess of everything, and we would throw ourselves on his mercy, and this is the tricky thing . . . I suppose we would expect him to forgive us, because that's our understanding of the father that forgives. And then, of course, we're wrestling with the fact that that might be a bit presumptuous.

So, I never know about this one. I know we've screwed up. I know we'd just ask for forgiveness. I know it would be given to us, but I can't be completely, totally certain that he'd forgive us, 'cause that would be presumptuous. But that's the little circle that Christians go round and round all the time, I guess. But, whatever, we would throw ourselves on his mercy.

OLIVIA: I don't think he'd sit down, clap his hands and say, 'This is just absolutely fantastic, well done!' I think he would chastise our congregation for our faith being too low, and not asking enough, not lifting our gaze enough, to him, for asking less and forgetting that he can do immeasurably more.

And I think that sometimes we pray, and we pray according to our vision of what we can see, rather than those big hairy audacious prayers that he sometimes wants us to pray, where we ask for something *completely* bizarre and left field and bonkers and watch God do it!

I think he would overturn our safety nets, if you like, and say, '*Just ask me!* Because I will give you what you ask for.' I mean, it does say God promises to give us the nations if we ask of him, and that he can do more than we ever ask or think. So, we need to ask more. And I think if he turned up, he would be saying, 'Come on congregation, I think you can do more.'

We're trying to impact our local area. And it's great to be able to do the same old things, hand out gospel tracts, you know, have events. But what if we ask God for more than, you know, what if there is more? What if we could just see through his eyes? I think he would say, 'Lift your gaze a little bit more.'

[13]
JERRY: On the theme of Good Samaritans in Luke and John's Gospel, who surprised our panel with friendship and support, and who have they surprised?

DAVID: I believe that we're always met by grace, all is grace, but grace comes from some surprising directions; it doesn't come from a direction you're expecting.

When Rachel and I got married – we'd been married for a year or so – and sadly she lost a baby. And in the middle of the parish, you know, all of a sudden, everybody comes to sympathize with you.

I have to say quite a lot of people who came, you know, they were of the 'never mind, better luck next time' variety, which wasn't really very helpful. But I used to take the assemblies in school, and there was a rough lad, who always used to talk to me after our assemblies, and he knocked on our door. And there he was, this rough lad in Middlesborough, holding a bunch of flowers.

And he said, 'Me mum sent these fur yer missus. I hopes she soon gets over her troubles.' And that was fantastic; it brought tears to my eyes! So, that surprised me. I think one, you know, prayer often we talk about self-examination. At the end of your day, don't beat yourself up, but ask yourself, what have people seen of Christ in me today? And what of Christ have I seen in others? Where have I been surprised? Where have I surprised people? End of.

BRENDAN: A big learning thing for me about friendship and support is that we learn the most from people who disagree with us.

I think a lot of people have told me this, that the people they expected to help them sometimes don't, and the people they didn't expect, the people maybe they didn't think were their friends, were the people who came to their aid, and certainly, in my profession, and working with people, that's something that I've always tried to bear in mind – that you learn more if you broaden up your table to take in people who disagree with you, you don't at first feel in sympathy with. Life becomes a lot richer. You learn a lot more. And you can be surprised by how kind and helpful people can be.

So, don't have too narrow sense of who your real friends are.

OLIVIA: I've always been surprised by a number of people. Perhaps the most people that have surprised me would be people who've not shared my faith at all – some who've been atheists, some who've been Muslims, who have been the people who've supported me, encouraged me in my faith. I'm thinking of one particular woman who just turned up to our church, out of the blue, a Muslim woman, who said, 'I wanted to see if there was faith out there. I'm a Muslim and I've got Muslim friends, but I wanted to see if Christians really believe what they say they believe.' And since her just turning up randomly, she has become a good friend and has been someone who's supported and championed me.

Now who have I surprised? It's very difficult to be able to answer that question really well. I've always been someone who's loyal. I think I'm a really good friend. And I'm always happy to demonstrate friendship because of the love of Christ in me. I'm always trying to be a good friend to somebody else. So, I suppose the answer to the question is to ask the people who I may have surprised.

[14]
JERRY: At the end of the session, we return to the woman caught in adultery, speculating whether she was the same woman of the Samaritan well. When the crowd is baying for blood, where do our panellists stand?

DAVID: Sometimes we need to have our nerve to stand against the pack. Often people hunt in packs. I've been to meetings, even at senior levels, and they'll go for somebody who isn't present and accuse them of being incompetent. And often I'll sort of stop and say, 'Look, hang on a minute. We're all incompetent. Who isn't incompetent? We're all incompetent.'

And so, having the nerve to go against the pack. I think, it comes from something that happened to me as a boy, in that I grew up in a tiny Yorkshire village where, in the sixteenth century, the lord of the manor had led a revolt really, a peaceful revolt against Henry the Eighth, closing down the monasteries. He'd taken Yorkshire and the north by storm, and think if he'd followed it up, he would have overthrown Henry the Eighth, which would have been a good thing in many ways. But he met with Henry's troops. And Aske far outnumbered them and agreed to terms, and they were false terms and Aske was executed. He's always been my sort of boyhood hero, and I'm called David and so, inevitably, I take on Goliaths who cross my path. Like Robert Aske.

BRENDAN: There's such a herd instinct in journalists, in people who report stories. They sniff out somebody that they want to attack, somebody obvious, who's screwed up . . . you know, Prince Andrew and that ridiculous interview . . . Matt Hancock, or whatever . . . And there's this media pile in, just the same way of the crowd baying for blood, and that's the . . . a good journalist just stands back when this herd instinct kicks in. And again, the secret, I think . . . get journalists who are what I would call contrarians. They see what the herd is doing, and they do the opposite and they make a reputation for that.

I think what's harder to do is neither follow the herd, nor be the reflex contrarian, but to be somebody who looks at what's happening, tells the reader what they see. Very difficult. But that,

I think, is the essence of a good writer, a good observer. You'll know from your work in journalism that telling the story straight, without pretending that you know it all and see everything, but to the best of your ability, telling people what happened here, that's a rare thing. And we don't get a lot of it at the moment. And it's such a precious part of the public square; people prepared to say what happened.

OLIVIA: When the crowd bays for blood, where do I stand? Well, obviously with my twenty-first century sensibilities, I wouldn't, I wouldn't be baying for her blood at all. But the grace with which Jesus and John recalls this story just shows just how much he loves – again we're talking about women – how much he loves this woman. I mean, she was condemned, wasn't she? She was caught in the act. But he turns it round because he loves her. He sees a situation, and, in turn, this woman becomes one of the most unlikeliest evangelists in the whole of Scripture. That tells me something about the love of Jesus to forgive, and to forgive the most heinous of crimes which, I suppose that would have been at that time.

JERRY: And that's the end of Session 3.

I WAS BLIND BUT NOW I SEE

JERRY: David writes that in Jesus' day, disability was seen as sent by God as punishment for some spiritual lapse. But does God cause or send suffering?

DAVID: When I was a boy, the Archbishop of York and then Canterbury was a guy called Michael Ramsay, who looked like a sort of teddy bear of a man really. And he was an eccentric. And they say that when he was first ordained, he went on a funeral visit, visiting somebody who's loved one had died. And he just went in and sat there for 40 minutes and didn't say a word.

And I think, well, that's not a bad thing really . . . to shut up in the face of terrible suffering rather than try to say something that makes it all alright, 'cause it never does.

And that's . . . you know, the questions you're asking about God – 'Where is God in suffering?' – those are big questions with no easy answers, and I sometimes think, if you come up with an easy answer or trite words, you're belittling the depth of suffering.

I think we're a society that's obsessed with post-mortems. Why did this happen? Why did that happen? Why did God do this? Why did you do that? I'd say, park the why, and instead replace it with what – what's God going to do now? Given that that's happened, what are you going to do now God? And I think then we move on; we take things forward.

BRENDAN: One of the things we learn from the Gospels is that God is in all things. Every joy, every mishap, every pain, every suffering, and we accept the life that we're in. We don't go chasing after pains or sufferings, but they're in every life, and that's the way the world is, which we know. I think one of the lessons from this broken world, with all this unimaginable and incomprehensible pain in it, is that when joy does come – which again it does in every life – that we seize it and settle back and relish it, and that when pain comes, we bear it, don't make too much of a fuss about it, we certainly never glory, just press on. But celebrate the good things when they're there, because we know that the suffering is going to come.

OLIVIA: I can only reflect upon what I believe around this. And that Jesus talks about it, in fact in John, John 16, that in this world, you'll have trouble. Trials are not uncommon; they're part of everyone's life. As hard as it is to accept, we can expect trials to be part of our lives. I think everyone that's listening to this will have had some degree of trials and/or suffering.

But I'm aware that also, in my most difficult times, where I have suffered and there has been physical pain and/or emotional pain accompanying that, that I feel that that's the time that I draw to God much closer. I know for some people, it may be something that actually drives them away from God. But for me, it's something that draws me to God, and I cling to God.

There is something about suffering that gives us a new perspective, and then, if it can be used, if we trust God and we believe that he is suffering, that he is suffering, that he helps us to take our eyes off our own personal suffering and to place them on Jesus.

So, in that, I think God both allows it, and possibly sends it too.

[16]
JERRY: What do the panellists think of healing on the Sabbath when doing things is forbidden?

DAVID: There's a lot of criticism levied at Jesus for healing on the Sabbath, but Jesus rounded on them and said, 'The Sabbath is made for man, not man for the Sabbath.'

And it's good to have a break. It's good to sort of take stock, catch your breath, recharge your batteries. That's very, very important. It's bad to be always doing. It's good to stop. But, if your house is on fire on the Sabbath, go for the hose pipe; don't think about how good it is to stop. You need to act. As St Augustine said, that when you're caught in a storm at sea, yes, do pray, but also row for the shore.

BRENDAN: I feel very guilty about this because I work every Sunday and every Bank Holiday, and we all need, we all need a break, we all need a rhythm where we're working and resting.

I'm 68. I've never really got into that rhythm. So, this is something, one of these many things about which I'm simply going to have to throw myself on the mercy of God. I should rest on a Sunday. It would be good for me, but I have to confess I don't.

OLIVIA: I think I adopt the same perspective as Jesus! Isn't that handy? Jesus seemed to – I wouldn't say he went out of his way to do it – but he certainly healed many people on the Sabbath. So, the man with the withered hand, the woman who was crippled with a disabling spirit, the man who had dropsy, my favourite, the healing of the man at the pool of Bethesda. And he knew the rules; he knew the Pharisees' rules regarding the Sabbath.

I think that in Jesus' case, he was thinking, 'Well, these people need healing. They need help.' Every time that he healed someone, he was always confronted by religious leaders of some description.

I love the way that he challenges them, and he says . . . he calls them hypocrites! Because he says, you know that I'm healing and you're coming at me, but if *you* had a donkey or an ox, that you knew was sick or needed water, you would lead it out to give it water, wouldn't you? So, I am doing exactly the same thing. So, why shouldn't I do that?

So, I think that Jesus in – I wouldn't say breaking the law but in fulfilling it – gives us permission to have another look at some of our religions that have so many rules attached to them, rules about doing and not rules about being . . . who are we to be as Jesus' representatives?

[17]
JERRY: The blind man's parents feared being kicked out of the synagogue. Their son was kicked out. Jesus was kicked

out of both the synagogue and the Holy City. Every club, even a religious club, has its membership rules. So, who's in and who's out of today's Church?

DAVID: There was an Archbishop of York and then Canterbury called William Temple, who was really the architect of the welfare state and the NHS. And he said that the Church was the only organization in history which existed for the benefit of those who were not its members . . . existed for the benefit of those who were not its members.

One of the things I like watching on television is saving lives at sea. What really impresses me is all these lifeboat crew, they never judge people for often getting in some ridiculous situations that are risking their lives and risking the lives of lifeboat crew. They never judge them; they rescue them. And that's what they're about. And I think really the only rule about a church is that lifeboat's the name and rescue is the game.

BRENDAN: Well, this inclusion agenda, if you want to call it that, is a big thing at the moment I think in all the churches. And nobody thinks that's a bad thing in itself, I don't think. But they would put more emphasis on having rules or guidelines that, if you want to join our club – we're not excluding anybody – if you want to join our club, these are the rules. If you follow them, you're in; if you don't, we'd rather you didn't come in.

And I think my feeling about this is that we tend . . . we do, we draw the lines in the wrong place. The borderlines between who is in and who is out; the map of the territory is . . . has got the borderlines written in the wrong place. And we think it's the borderline between those who are doing the right thing, following certain rules, the people who are righteous, and people who are sinful or falling down – they're outside, not in the territory. And the only borderline that matters isn't between the good/the perfect and the people that are screwing up, the people that are sinful – it's between the people who are forgiving, listened, who were curious, who got a sense of wonder of things, and people who think they're saved, or they're right, or there are rules they want to follow.

And I want them to come in as well. But it's the people who don't see grace outside this club that they're in, don't see God outside the club they're in, who don't understand that other people's story is just as interesting as their own. That's where the borderline should be insofar as you can call it a borderline. It's a borderline that goes across everybody's heart. It's not between us and them; it's between a bit of us and another bit of us.

OLIVIA: I think it's dependent upon the denomination of the church. So, some churches, by the very tenets of their denomination, is more conservative and others are much more liberal.

It would be almost impossible for me to say who's in and who's out . . . Coming from a conservative church, a more conservative setting, I know that some of the things that we battle with – not because people are out because we love all people – but some of the areas that some of our denominations and denomination and denominations – we're not the only ones that battle with – are areas where people are transgender, so LGBQT+? We also have some issues with women, about their equality with men and their equality with men as ministers and as leaders of congregations, and of having a voice. People of colour, for example. Some churches struggle with what equality means, although they'll say it by words, their actions speak something . . . say something completely different.

And this one is a sad one, and it's about, you know, some people who are out maybe in some of our conservative churches. Our churches tend towards favouring those of middle classes? And the higher or lower socioeconomic groups and groups where the poor predominantly reside, the marginalized . . . maybe some of those who are 'out' in our common parlance, although we purport to be inclusive, sometimes our actions are exclusive.

[18]
JERRY: Reflecting on John's healing of the man born blind, David stresses the irony that those who could see – the religious experts of the day – were blind to Jesus. So, what is the Church of today blind to?

DAVID: There was a little poem by Thomas Hardy that he wrote in 1924, if I may quote it to you. It's not a long poem, so worry not.

> 'Peace upon earth!' was said. We sing it,
> And pay a million priests to bring it.
> After two thousand years of mass
> We've got as far as poison-gas.

So, there you go. I think we all sort of neglect Christ and are blind to him. He said, 'Love your enemies do good to those who hate you.' 'Those who live by the sword shall die by the sword.' We turn a blind eye to all of that, and so, yeah, we're all guilty of it and we all need to read the gospel afresh and take it to heart.

There's a famous writer, author of the Father Brown books, the mystery and the detective books, C. K. Chesterton, who said, 'It's not that Christianity has been tried and found wanting. It's never been tried.'

Open our eyes, so we're not blind to Christ.

BRENDAN: I get my experiences as a journalist, as somebody who's putting together every week a story of what's happening in the world. And what's happening outside in the Church is that we're blind to how wicked we are; how much sinfulness there is in the Church. And we're blind to how much glory and sacrifice and goodness, greatness there is in the Church and in the world outside. That we're always looking for the pure and the impure, the righteous and the damned, and they're all here under our nose, in our own hearts, in our own church. And I think that's the thing that we often don't see. We don't see the grace in ourselves, and we don't see the grace outside ourselves.

OLIVIA: It would be really pretentious of me to be able to speak for the Church – big C or little c, really. However, there are some things that are common that I think that the Church needs to wake up to, whether it's blind to it or not, I'm unable to say that. I know that some churches may be, but I am concerned about the disunity, and increasing fractiousness of churches around, along the lines of denomination and denominationalism, and that, although we all want to belong to a particular tribe, that it actually mitigates against Jesus' saying, 'that they all may be one as we are one'. Over the centuries, since Jesus said that we've fractured into *thousands, thousands* of little denominations, and the disunity that we face, divided against, you know, with certain doctrines, what do you believe about this or that?

I think the Church of today needs to be . . . the veil needs to be taken away from our eyes so that we can start to work together. Because I believe that there is more that unites us than divides us.

JERRY: And that's the end of Session 4.

[19]
Session 5
THEM BONES, THEM BONES, THEM DRY BONES

JERRY: David began this session recalling the four readings he chose to read at assembly as a school prefect in Hull. But which four would he and the other panellists choose now?

DAVID: I think my first choice would be the book of Ruth, a wonderful book about a Gentile widow, whose faithfulness enables her to be the grandmother of King David, Israel's greatest king, and Jesus, of course, son of David. And it's Ruth faithfulness, even to a mother-in-law, of all people, 'Wherever you go, I will go.'

My second choice would be the book of Song of Songs because it makes God out to be sexy, when the Church hides that rather well! But it's celebrating love really, erotic love, but there's some lovely lines there if I could just quote you a line. 'Wear me as a seal upon your heart, for love is as strong as death; many waters cannot quench love; no flood can sweep it away.'

My third choice would be something I've read at every funeral I've ever taken in 41 years ministry, Romans 8, 'Nothing can separate us from love of God in Christ Jesus our Lord.' Nothing in all creation could separate us from Jesus.

And finally, what text would I go for? I think I go for John, chapter 20, which I've read out on every Easter day since I was ordained, that wonderful story where Mary is by the tomb weeping, and Jesus, who she thinks is the gardener, but he isn't, Jesus says to her, 'Mary.' And she turns and says to him, 'Rabboni.' 'My master.' Hardly any script there, 'Mary.' 'My master.' But it always brings tears to my eyes because it's the best script in the world.

BRENDAN: When I read that story, I started to think about what the four would be. And again, that's the moment when the editor kicks in, and I immediately thought, 'Let's invite people to decide what their four stories is, their four favourite stories would be. Let's have a poll. Let's have a competition. Let's have a list.' So, the instinct is always to see a moment like that. There's an opportunity to bring your readers in, include people.

So, and I notice that David actually only had three stories, and I think you've spun one of them over two days, in stretching things a bit there. So, that's what I would do in that circumstance. I would turn it around, in the way editors do, rather than pontificate to their readers. We're going to have a competition. And invite readers to tell us what the four most telling gospel stories are.

OLIVIA: My four would be Exodus 33, 12 to 23. And it's where Moses is asking God to show him his glory. I love that, I think that's beautiful. Won't expand on it any further. The second one is 2 Timothy 1, verse 7, where Paul is advocating Timothy, timid Timothy: 'For God has not given us a spirit of fear but of power, love and self-discipline.' I suppose I like that because I'm a classic introvert. So, the spirit of fear and timidity always used to resonate with me quite a lot.

My other reading would be in John 9, where Jesus heals the man who's born blind. I love the exchange between the man who's born blind – all he cares about is that he can now see! – and the fact that the Pharisees have brought, wheeled his parents in to find out, what's going on here? I love that. That would be one of my readings. And the other one is, and my last one, is Luke 5, verses 1 to 11, where the disciples have fished all night and caught nothing, and then Jesus says, 'Just go on the other side of the boat.' It's like . . . that is just crazy! I just love, I just love that. It speaks of possibilities to me. Of what Jesus does, even though you've done everything that he says, and he just says, 'Just try it this way.'

[20]
JERRY: David says in his text that when Jesus, the living water, cries over dead Lazarus, he gives dignity to tears. By inhabiting a human life, what other emotions or activities does the Son of God give dignity to?

DAVID: Well, 'Jesus wept.' is the shortest verse in the Bible, just two words, but it's got the greatest significance, as I say, giving dignity to tears. And I think Jesus, by living amongst us, gives dignity to all of it. Because we're all prone to beat ourselves up. You know, I'm very bad. I'm a man. And men are toxic, aren't they? So, I'm very bad to start with. I'm also a priest and a bishop, and they're very bad people. And I'm a very bad husband. And a very bad father.

And you know, the media can make you have a real down on yourself. You feel very bad. Whereas Jesus came to make us feel good about ourselves. He said in John's Gospel, 'I have come to bring life in all its fullness so that you may have joy.'

So go for joy. I heard about an old couple who used to have hanging in their bedroom over the bedhead, 'The Lord thy God seeth thee and judgeth thee', which must have been quite a downer for their lives really.

But I'd replace it with the text that you may have joy, that you may have joy. And if people went through their days thinking that, life would be a lot different.

BRENDAN: I think one of the greatest gifts of all is the gift of tears, and again if you're in storytelling in journalism, writing about what's happened in the Church over the last 20, 25 years, especially the sexual abuse, what we know about violence against women . . . Last few months we've had the blasphemy of Christian leaders describing, talking of the holy war.

There's so much that's wrong and cause of shame, and the only response is not to explain it away or defend it; you have to be honest about it, talk about it. But first, I sometimes think, is just to sit quietly and to cry. That gift of tears before we wipe our tears and get on with the job of putting things right. Being honest about it; it's just such a lovely moment. I'm really grateful to David for just noticing that, because the big drama is the bringing back of Lazarus to life. Beautiful. But that little throw away – he cried. Good thing to cry sometimes.

OLIVIA: Yeah, I think Jesus gives dignity to passion and indignation, and I'm thinking about when he was angry and he overthrew the Temple, the tables of, sorry, of commerce in the Temple. And I'm also thinking of Jesus when he talks about his amazement when this centurion has a servant who needs healing, and he sends to Jesus and says to Jesus: 'You know, you don't have to come; just say the word and he'll be healed.'

And Jesus says that 'I'm amazed! I'm amazed at this centurion, who has people under him and is a leader, for saying, I don't need to come; just say the word.' He's amazed and he tells the crowd that 'I tell you that I haven't seen faith like this in all Israel'.

So, the fact that Jesus shows amazement, he shows . . . he cries . . . as we've talked about, and also that he gives dignity and is passionate and angry, I think those are other ways that shows us the humanity of Jesus.

[21]
JERRY: David wonders whether Jesus is angry at nature, red in tooth and claw, but only the fittest survive. What has the Christian gospel to say about evolution? David and Brendan answer this.

DAVID: Well, I think the survival of the fittest is a trend, you know, it's a trend there in creation, and we can't buck that. But human beings don't necessarily go with the trend. We shape our environment, rather than are shaped by it. If we're cold, if we're freezing, we don't freeze to death, we light a fire. Okay, that causes global warming, as it doesn't always work out that well, but we do shape, we're shapers rather than shaped.

And so, yes, survival of fittest is there. But we don't have to go with that. And I think the theory of evolution clashes with the Bible, not because of Genesis and all that version of creation there. I think it clashes with the Bible because of Jesus' Passion, trial and death, which is about the survival of the weakest.

A poor little man nailed up on a cross is hailed as God's son, and God moves mightily and resurrects him. And so, thereby proclaiming the survival of the weakest. So, it's an interesting, an interesting sort of two theories grating together.

BRENDAN: My children and my wife are descended from Charles Darwin. So, my wife was brought up in a very secular environment as a proud Darwinian, and she's now become a faithful Christian and she's no less a proud Darwinian. So, I've learnt from her faith and her life you can combine evolution with Christian faith. And I know because I've seen it done.

[22]
JERRY: David quotes Michael Sheen, ending his Port Talbot Passion play with the words, 'Now it begins'. Is Easter the be all and end all of our faith or just the start of things?

DAVID: I think it's both. They say, 'New every morning', don't they, a fresh slate. And I think what gets me going in the morning is that I believe in Easter, I believe everything is resurrectable. I'm not a bishop or a priest who thinks of himself as an expert on faith. I'm not an expert. I'm more of a sort of adventurer really, a detective, and I go out every day, I go every day, looking for Christ. I've got an identikit picture in the Gospels, and I go out looking for him. And boy, do I find him in some surprising places! Occasionally, very occasionally, I even find him in the Church.

BRENDAN: I think the Passion, the death and the resurrection, all that despair, and all that hope, we've got to keep them all together. We don't kind of leave them behind. So, when he comes back onto the stage and announces, declares that now it begins, I think you have to keep all those things together. So, we dress ourselves down, we wipe those tears away. And then we get on with the job.

We don't forget the tears, and I think in that spirit, that message, we wake up, we brush ourselves down, we start again, but we don't forget. We carry those tears and those wounds with us.

OLIVIA: I'm going to cop out and say it's both. So, Easter is for me, the 'so what?' of my faith, because it feels like it's a marker. Jesus has died. Jesus is now, is resurrected, and that's, it's like a comma in a sentence for me, in an unfinished sentence.

So, what does this mean to me? And it feels as if, it's a way of God saying, 'Now you write your story because I am resurrected; I am the resurrection life. And I'm promising you eternal life. What are you going to do about it? What's the soul? What for you?'

It's a marker for me that challenges me with a question, 'What will my story be because of the Easter story? What do I write in between the commas there?' And I have to fill in the blank. And so, for me, it is the be all that end all of my faith, but it's also the start of new things as well.

JERRY: That's the end of Session 5 and the end of our course. Thanks so much to David, Olivia and Brendan for their lively contributions. Thank you for taking part.

I hope you have both enjoyed and been disturbed by meeting Jesus afresh in John's Gospel. Wherever you are, we wish you a holy Easter and, in the final words of that Port Talbot Passion play, 'Now it begins'.